Productivity: 15 Simple Tips to Get Things Done with Passion and Speed

By Suzie Carr

Copyright © 2016, Suzie Carr. All rights reserved. This book, or parts thereof, may not be reproduced in any form without permission from the publisher.

Novels by Suzie Carr:
The Fiche Room
Two Feet off The Ground
Tangerine Twist
Inner Secrets
A New Leash on Life
The Muse
Staying True
Snowflakes
The Journey Somewhere
Sandcastles
The Dance

How-to Books by Suzie Carr:
Writer's Insights
18 Simple Writing Tips to Create Memorable Characters: Writing Made Easy

Keep up on Suzie's latest news and projects:
www.curveswelcome.com

Follow Suzie on Twitter:
@girl_novelist

For anyone who has a goal to achieve.

Acknowledgements

I want to thank my sister, Debra, for her help with beta reading this book and providing insightful feedback. I also want to thank my friend, April, for her support and constant encouragement. To my editor, JoAnn, your guidance is always appreciated! I always learn a great deal from your honest suggestions. Finally, I'd like to thank the many people who continue to support my efforts and teach me some of life's most valuable lessons!

Contents

First Things First 1
Tip #1: Get Organized 7
Tip #2: Start Saying No 13
Tip #3: Stop Waiting for the Perfect Moment 23
Tip #4: Create a Ritual 31
Tip #5: Discover Time-Wasters 37
Tip #6: Develop Self-Control 47
Tip #7: Set Goals 53
Tip #8: Key in on Your Highest Value Activities . 65
Tip #9: Focus on the Task at Hand 71
Tip #10: Think Small, Digestible Steps 77
Tip #11: Create a Deadline 81
Tip #12: Nurture Your Health 87
Tip #13: Take a Nap 97
Tip #14: Find the Key Ingredient 103
Tip #15: Know Your "Why" 113
Conclusion 119
Works Cited 125
Index 126

First Things First

Life is going to toss some tough obstacles in the way from time to time, and these serve to remind that we have lessons to learn and important things to do. We're not put on this earth to merely survive. We are here to thrive. We are meant for greatness.

That being said, to achieve any amount of this greatness, we must push forward and stay focused. We can't rely on luck to lift us to our potentials. We must dig deep to find our grit, that power inside that burns thick and hot, fueling our desires and allowing for wins when temptations surround us.

If you've got a dream to get to the next level, to pursue that passion, to get off the current path and onto one that shines with the promise of a brighter future, then you must stay focused and determined.

In this technological age of smartphones and interesting gadgets, it's easy to get lost and find ourselves stuck in the muck of the worn-out rat race where dreams and passions go to die. It requires an unwavering, conscientious effort to stay the course and get things done.

If this intimidates you, it should. If it didn't, life would be a ginormous bore.

Critical Element to Productivity

The one critical element of staying productive on your pursuit of greatness in any endeavor is a burning desire, and the catalyst to that desire is escaping the trap of complacency. The more comfortable we feel, the more apt we are to stay exactly where we are in life. I don't know about you, but the thought of that terrifies me because this would mean I've stopped growing.

We're meant to grow. We're meant to water the garden of our intellect and talent and watch it emerge from the depths of impossibility to the heights of opportunity.

If you desire to live your greatest life, then you must be willing to change and tweak, constantly refining your process as you learn better ways of doing things. To get to this state of mind, you must be focused and willing.

Why a Book on Productivity?

I decided to write this book because I've found myself in that line of overwhelming distraction and said, "No way!" to it. I've got way too much to do in this life, and procrastination has no place in it. I've been bitten by that bug before, and nothing pretty resulted. Projects failed to get off the ground. Opportunities appeared and vanished on a hissing shout. Regrets piled up and cluttered my view. I finally got fed up and got to work analyzing my weaknesses and researching ways to thrive instead of just survive.

A little about me: I work full-time as a content digital specialist in a very busy marketing department at a university, and I also write novels, blog weekly, promote my work through social media, and try to get adequate sleep, exercise, nutrition and quality time with both my better half and lovable dog, Bumblebee.

Phew, typing all that just made me tired!

Succeeding at these things in life takes diligence and a keen eye on the end value of the effort. Many people ask me how I'm still sane. My answer to them is that I've learned a thing or two about setting expectations, and how by setting them just right, I am able to stay productive and in flow.

I used to stretch myself too thin, so much that I ended up with a few health issues that ultimately knocked some sense back into me.

The Healthy Side of Productivity

Being productive to me means being healthy at the end of any given day. Too many times, we burn that candle on both ends only to find ourselves unable to lift our head off the pillow, never mind accomplish anything meaningful.

Here's the deal – as human beings we have a great capacity to emerge as success stories, and this capacity grows the more thoughtful we are in our actions.

Most reading this could likely fill a notebook with things they need to do in a day's time. We've got meals to plan, plants to water, dependents to care for, dust to swipe away, bills to pay, calls to make, email to check, Facebook statuses to write, etc. Now imagine if you want to advance in your career, start a relationship, or open a business? How do you get it all done and protect yourself from shutdown?

Let's face it, when you become flustered and overwhelmed by commitments, a natural response is often procrastination. It's easier to put things aside and deal later.

Please understand: there's a better way!

Why Read This Book?

If you suffer from the endless barrage of distractions, demands, pings and alerts from your smartphone, and tend to put aside ideas for things you'd love to do because you have no time to consider them, then this book is for you.

Now more than ever before, we need to find ways to organize so we ride through the distractions and realize our dreams.

Read on if you want to learn the top 15 tips I've discovered to stay productive and focused, even under the most extreme pressures.

Tip #1: Get Organized

Clutter is like the sneaky cold virus that comes in on a whisper. At first, you don't notice its entrance. It hides in the quiet recesses of the unnoticed, slowly building on itself until it gets nice and comfy. Then it begins to multiply, stretching beyond natural, taking over territories not able to coexist peacefully in its presence. Before long, it clouds the once pure space that offered tranquility and rest. It thrives in the new chaos it forms, casting upon us an obnoxious force that inevitably overruns the very environment we need to sustain our focus, health, and overall quality of life.

Clutter Gets in the Way

Clutter tempts us to procrastinate. It beckons us

to focus on what's around us instead of what's right smack-dab in front. Clutter is like a clogged highway. It doesn't allow for freedom of movement. Horns are beeping, tempers are flaring, and we're just idle, unable to get away from the mess. We can't accelerate. We can't flee the scene. We are prisoners to the limitations set by the conditions. No matter how much we focus on getting out of the madness, we simply cannot. We've left no room to circumvent the charged emotions or the pileup of excess. We find ourselves stuck in the middle of the crazed chaos, and unless we choose to forgo the similar roadways in the future, we're at risk of losing ground on our pursuits. As clutter progresses, we digress.

Clutter is toxic. It eats away at our prolific intentions. It covers us in a film of weariness and frustration that clouds our creative ingenuity.

Clutter enters into our life in many forms. It can be in the form of low-yield tasks, physical stuff, emotional demands placed on us, or even constant worry over things way outside of our control.

We allow clutter in for many reasons. We may

find comfort in keeping things, afraid to let them go for sentimental or practical reasons. We may want to please people and not disappoint them by saying no to their demands. We may expect too much of ourselves and overcommit to tasks. We may be incessant worriers who fear losing control over a situation if we stop thinking about it.

Whatever the reason for letting clutter in, we have to understand that it impedes on our ability to be clear and focused.

Neuroscientists at Princeton University studied the differences of people's task performance in an organized versus disorganized environment. The results showed that clutter competes for your attention, resulting in decreased performance and increased stress.

So what can you do?

Give away an item daily or weekly
Go around your space and tune into the clutter. Find an item and ask yourself if it brings value to your life. If no, give it away, sell it, or recycle it.

Fill a recycle bag

Select an area in your home for a recycle bag. Set a goal to fill that bag weekly with items that no longer add value to your life. Your brain will go on a hunt for items it can use to fill that bag. We are programmed to succeed. We want to fill that bag!

Try the Oprah Winfrey closet hanger experiment

Oprah introduced us to someone's brilliant idea when it comes to clearing wardrobe clutter. Hang all your clothes with the hangers in the reverse direction. After you wear an item, return it to the closet with the hanger facing the correct direction. After six months, you'll have a clear picture of which clothes you can easily donate.

This technique also works great for other items in the house. Apply it to toys. Place a sticker on each toy, place them all on a shelf with the sticker facing the wall. After your child plays with them, return it with the sticker facing away from the shelf wall. After six months, you'll know which toys to donate.

Don't stop there. You can also apply this concept

to baseball hats, everyday shoes, and folded t-shirts in a drawer.

Create a room list

Take some time to draft a list of specific rooms and areas within your home or office that need decluttering. Before I decluttered, my pantry scared me most of all. I hated going into it because I knew my brain would hurt. Over the years, I'd pile things onto shelves and close the door. Well, over time, you can imagine the mess. I dreamed of having a pantry that I could open and see every item. I wanted canned goods to be in one area, not hidden behind bags of flour that expired two years prior. That cluttered pantry took the joy out of cooking.

Determine which areas of your life need organization by figuring out where the mental and physical drains lurk.

After you've made your list, commit to tackling one space a week.

Get a new view

I always say that my house is cleanest right before I'm expecting company. This is when I go into ultra-organizing mode. I look around my house and think, well that's embarrassing! I view my home from the perceived perspective of the visitor and am able to see things I don't normally see. That pile of extra pillows and blankets I shoved into the corner of the spare bedroom no longer seems fitting when my best friend is going to see it.

Play frugal consumer

Go around your house and analyze items from the view of a frugal consumer. Ask yourself questions like, how much would I pay for this? If I saw this on a store shelf today, would I buy it? Would I give this item to someone as a gift? When you start to ask yourself questions like this, you are inviting in truthful answers. Your answers should help you determine which items are clutter and which ones still hold value.

Tip #2: Start Saying No

I used to have a heck of a time saying no to people. It didn't matter if I shared the same bloodline as them or never even met face-to-face, the burden of turning someone away who needed my help tormented me. I had always been of the mindset that I must serve others to experience purpose and deservedness. To turn away when someone asked for my help seemed wrong on so many levels. What if the person needed me, and by turning her down I set her up to fail? I couldn't live with myself if I did that to someone. Well, that line of thinking, in all its generosity and selflessness, slowly began to undermine my opportunity of getting ahead, and thus being able to serve in a greater capacity.

What You Allow in Stays in

Speaking in general terms, people will continue to ask you to stop everything you are doing to help them solve a problem if you allow it. The more you abandon your plans for theirs, the more they will take advantage of your generosity.

It's hard to look someone in the eyes and say no. I can tell you, though, it's even harder to live with the regrets of failed projects and dreams as a result of giving in to someone's pleading.

Despite what we are taught, it is okay to say no to those things that are not in alignment with our purpose. If we can learn to do this, we can go to the places we are meant to go in life.

It's no surprise that the more we say yes to other people's priorities, the less we say yes to our own. The result, also not surprising, is a massive debt in the pursuit of our dreams. What we deem important and essential falls to the wayside, and we begin to starve our needs to feed someone else's. When we place ourselves at the bottom of the barrel, we lose grip on what's important to us.

The truth of the matter is, we can't be two places at one time. We can't fill our plate past capacity and expect nothing to fall off. We can't dig ourselves into a hole and expect to climb up when we're pointed downward.

When We Say Yes

Imagine for a moment, if you will, a tomato plant. To bring it to life, you plant it in nourishing soil, equally spaced apart from all the other garden plants to ensure it has the range of motion it'll need to grow into the superstar tomato producer you envision. As it starts to grow, you keep it aligned towards the sky by propping it up against wooden stakes, allowing the stakes to support its strong stems, and future strong fruit. After about a month, you begin to see a cute little shoot popping up beside it. Their fresh green color adds beauty to the garden. You whisper to yourself, *eh, that's harmless*. Instead of saying no to their presence, you allow them to fill in the area around the tomato plant. After all, they are quite beautiful with their delicate stems and cheery heart-shaped leaves.

A few days pass, and you notice the cute little leaves are beginning to wrap themselves around your tomato plant. In fact, they look as though they are strangling your tomato plant. They are taking over the ground, the stake, the entire plant! Your plant can no longer thrive because it's taking on the burden of this weed. By saying yes, the tomato plant's resources to water and space have been undermined. Your plant is in jeopardy of losing its place in the garden because you couldn't say no to that cute little innocent shoot.

That weed can thrive in many conditions. It does not need the tomato plant to survive. It saw an opportunity to grow at the expense of another, and took it. Why wouldn't it? The real casualty here is that neither one needed the other to thrive. One didn't necessarily serve the other. It just so happened the invite extended itself, and it seemed a waste to not accept it.

Innocent requests from people are a lot like that weed. Under the right circumstances, people will take up root where they are welcomed. If never turned away, they will keep right on requesting. Before long, many of us become that tomato plant, vying for resources we need to grow.

Are We Being Selfish?

As a society, we are programmed to be helpful, contributing whenever possible to the greater good. We're told we're less selfish when we put others before ourselves. But, in taking a closer look, when you put others before yourself, you are telling the world that your dreams come secondary. When we place our dreams in this fallout position, we'll never realize them. They will become victims of the dangerous circumstance of neglecting our God-given gifts for the sake of being a good, giving member of society.

When we fail to light the fire under our dreams, we fail to share gifts that could help lift and inspire others. If we're always chasing the tail of someone else's dream, as a society, we'll get nowhere fast, running in circles.

We have to believe that our work matters. We have been given a set of gifts, skills, talents, and we should fully embrace them by nurturing them. Sometimes this means having to say the dreaded word – no!

By not saying no, you're letting others uproot your chance of molding your gifts into something magical. When we are aligned with our passions, we are more productive. If we're constantly pushing our passions to the side to cater to someone else's, we are not bringing the best of ourselves into this world. Therefore, the argument of self-serving by saying no voids itself. By continually saying yes, we are being selfish because we are removing the chance for our gifts to take up flight and positively affect the world around us.

We Need Boundaries

We owe it to ourselves to set boundaries. Without them, people are going to walk all over our dreams, squashing them with no mercy just so they can serve themselves. They will burst right into your life and chisel away at your plans.

The more you say yes, the more demanding they will become.

Handling this kind of situation comes down to a question: *does this add value to my life?*

Saying no is hard. We want to appear amenable, reliable, and dependable. We want to be liked. We fear that by saying no, we risk losing respect and friendship. We're also afraid to miss out on opportunities.

But here's the thing: Saying yes may result in saying no to something more valuable.

You can't let everything in and expect to be open to new opportunities. Saying yes to too many things throws us off balance. It's counterproductive, not to mention, overwhelming.

How to Begin Saying No

Don't answer right away
Allow for some breathing room whenever asked to help with something outside the scope of your

priorities. Cement this rule into your life. This will open up space to weigh the options and consequences before committing or not.

Example: "Thanks so much for thinking of me. I'd like to look at my schedule, and I'll get back to you tomorrow to let you know."

Be concise

Saying no often leads a person down that guilty path where she looks for ways to soften the blow. This typically comes in the form of excuses, over generalizations, even lies. Keep your answer short and to the point. You don't have to offer a reason for saying no.

Example: "I'm sorry, but at this time I can't commit to xyz. I've got a lot on my plate at the moment. I'm grateful you thought of me in the first place."

Minimize guilt

I'll again suggest you ask yourself this question: Does this add value? If the answer is no, then guilt has no place in your heart.

Analyze your feelings

If you are volunteering to do something and it feels like an arduous chore, you are not going to derive joy from it. If you don't enjoy something, that emotion will seep into all involved. Do you want to spread that kind of vibe?

Create rules and stick to them

Create a process for determining what you agree and disagree to and stick to it. People will treat you the way you allow them to treat you. If you let them barge into your life with demands, and drop everything to cater to them, they will expect this every time. Set boundaries you can live with, and don't allow any breaches to them.

Let others know what they can expect from you. If they want you available for an evening phone call, and it's not what you want, be straightforward and set the rule that you are a morning person, and evenings are off limits. No excuses. Just plain and simple honesty.

Learning to say no becomes easier with time and practice. If something doesn't lead you towards your dreams, create happiness, or aid in your grand plan, let it go. The less you have to carry on your journey, the more adventurous you can be!

Tip #3: Stop Waiting for the Perfect Moment

No matter how much we try, we can never be fully prepared. So, if you're waiting for all the stars to be aligned in just the right position before you move, you could end up digging yourself into a hole and be pummeled with regret. Waiting on the perfect moment wastes valuable time. For every second you're not doing something, you're getting further away from what you desire.

Let's look at an example. Let's say you're going on a camping trip. It's smart to plan thoroughly, of course. Part of the planning process consists of taking the time to pack essentials like rain gear, proper shoes, matches, sleeping bags, and sun protectant. If you get stuck too long in the planning process, you'll miss the entire trip. You can be prepared for hurricanes, floods, sun-scorching temps, and it won't matter if you never take that car out of park and put the pedal to the metal.

At some point, you've got to shift the car into drive and trust you've done enough.

Trusting oneself is hard to do for many. Once you've rounded the corner out of your neighborhood and begin to travel down the interstate doing sixty-five, it'll be difficult to brake and turn around because you forgot something. It would be difficult on an emotional level because once you start the process towards momentum, you don't want to stop. You want to keep on driving until you get to your destination. You know deep down that you will be able to get creative on how to replace that thing you forget once you pitch your tent, ignite the smoldering fire, and get the meat sizzling on the grill.

A wonderful thing happens when we start the engine and accelerate away from the waiting position. Something clicks in our brain that creates a strong resistance against going back to the starting point. We'd rather circle the globe than retrace our steps. We want to keep moving forward and embrace that intense and supercharged tingle of progress, despite any obstacle that gets in the way.

The more we experience this effect, the more we crave it, and the less apt we are to stand naked at the foot of the journey clinging to our fears like a child to her blanket.

Get Uncomfortable

The greatest gift you can give to yourself when facing an uncertain outcome is to get comfortable being uncomfortable. As long as you are uncomfortable, you are not going to sit idle. You are going to do what you have to do to find new ground. In other words, you are going to move and not wait for things to align perfectly.

Here's the truth, you'll never be 100% ready. Fear captures everyone. So, how will you deal with the fear? To sit in comfort is so easy as we toss out excuses like confetti as to why we can't move forward. The sun isn't shining bright enough. The road is too wet. Storm clouds are brewing.

Unless you're in the threat zone of heading straight into the vortex of a tornado or similar scary weather phenomenon, you have no excuse to wait for the perfect moment. Get out there and get wet or get stuck in the muck of apprehension.

Twists and turns fill our lives. At any moment, a challenge can come straight out of nowhere and knock us off our feet. You can prepare until you are out of breath, and it won't matter. So, with this in mind, why wait when we never know how life will blindside us from one moment to the other anyway?

None of us come equipped with special eyes that can see clearly into the future. None of us know what the hell we're truly getting ourselves into in the grand scheme of things. So sure, we're going to have doubts.

With so much uncertainty, logic tells us then, that perfect moments don't exist.

So the question becomes, what the heck are we waiting for?

Don't wait for the perfect moment. Get out there and enjoy the thrills, the twists & turns and surprises of each brand new day.

Why Wait?

When we wait too long to move, we not only get stuck, we start to get paranoid. We start overanalyzing things to the point no idea seems good enough anymore. This happened to me on more than one occasion when writing a novel.

I used to think I had to have the story plan perfect before I could write a word of my novel. This just set me up for massive failure and disappointment because I'd set these unrealistic expectations of what the landscape of my literary world needed to look like before I could type a single key. I shudder at the thought of how many lost characters, ideas, and witty snippets of dialogue I missed out on because of my need to wait for perfection to set in before taking action.

The way out of such an idealistic mindset is to command yourself to get uncomfortable. Allow yourself free reign to mess up. With that kind of freedom, anything is possible.

When I had set out to write my ninth novel, *Sandcastles*, I did so with this exact mindset. After doing exhaustive research on holistic medicine and psychic abilities, I sat down to plot my story. Jitters sprung because I stressed about my story not being in perfect alignment with my original plan. So, you know what I did? I commanded myself to sit in a chair with a pad and pen and go off on a tangent. I journaled as my main character, ignoring the story plan. The result: my character took my story in a whole new direction, a much better direction than I could've come up with using my anal rules!

I dug deep into her psyche, getting uncomfortable with the unconventional approach, and came out a winner. I wrote that book in record time, refusing to sit in the waiting position. No, I took that pen, pressed it onto that paper, and took action.

When you set your expectations to be perfect, you will ultimately murder your dreams.

Perfection is Not Real

Perfection is a road block set up to force us into an idle position.

Rev up your engine, go around that roadblock,

and let loose on those dreams.

Screw perfection.

If you've got a burning desire, you don't have time to be perfect.

I'm not advising that you shouldn't strive for excellence. There's a huge difference between seeking perfection and putting out our best. Putting out our best means putting it out there and learning from it. Take all the feedback and lessons, be responsive, and search for ways to improve and reshape.

That's getting it done. And the more you get it done, the better you'll become at understanding what doesn't work and what does.

Tip #4: Create a Ritual

We've all heard how one bad move in the morning can create a snowball effect throughout our day. Say you stub your toe on your way into the bathroom first thing. You probably will fear the rest of your day is going to take a sharp turn downhill, and fast. This does seem to be the case. We wake up on the wrong side of the bed and spend the rest of the day in one long trudge to nightfall.

What you do in the morning sets the tone for the rest of your day. If you read or listen to interviews of successful people, you will hear a similar beat to their advice. They will tell you it's what they do in the morning that jumpstarts their productivity for the day. If you have a positive experience in the morning, you are more likely to carry that throughout every action of your day. So, it's important to advise here that if you wake up on the wrong side of the bed, reset yourself to a more positive vibe. I find a gratitude list is helpful. I read it to get back onto a frequency that is positive.

A Prelude to Success

You want to set yourself up for success. How can you do this best? Remember that we are the sum of our choices. What we do today affects us tomorrow. As human beings, we are programmed to seek out habits and structure. We crave the stability of knowing what's expected.

Surprises are nice in life. They keep us on our toes. But, when it comes to important aspects of life, a system can be the difference between success and failure. Operating within structure helps us to organize our patterns in a logical, clear, and manageable way. For instance, our morning routines allow us to sail through important steps to get us out of bed and out of the door in an organized, non-stressful way. We emerge from our restful slumbers renewed and ready to tackle the day. Our morning ritual sets us up for success.

Having a set ritual keeps your brain focused by wiping out unnecessary stresses. Rituals will enhance your ability to reinforce positive behavior.

Rituals can play a huge role in your success by freeing up your mind from the stress of the unknowns to be better equipped to handle those all-important surprises of creativity and innovation.

Rituals serve a similar purpose of a coach. They keep us on track. They ensure that we're hitting the important marks of things we might otherwise put aside, like nutrition, stretching, clearing the mind, and de-stressing.

Rituals remind us to pause, reflect and recharge.

Examples of empowering daily rituals:
- Yoga stretches first thing in the morning.
- Drinking lemon water upon waking.
- Drinking a green smoothie to lift your mood, mental functioning, and immune system.
- Reviewing your daily goals.

- Deep breathing every hour.
- 50 minutes of hard, focused work. 10 minutes of rest. Repeat.
- When eating a meal, eat the meal. No distraction. No email. No cell phone. No television. Eat the meal and savor it.
- Ask yourself at the end of the day: What important lesson did I learn today?

Task-shifting rituals are powerful.

I break into a series of 10 quick shoulder rolls followed by ten quick arm swings before any writing session. My mental energy shifts. This exercise releases tension. It tells my brain, it's time to write now. This ritual gets my brain off any other thoughts and onto the path of creativity.

I find that task-shifting rituals like this help to get me out of the grind and muck. Somewhere in the wind that I create with each rotation of my arm, exists a force that expels negative thoughts. I like to imagine that the air circulating within those rotations becomes supercharged with all these cool ions that become the positive catalysts to inspired thoughts.

Task-shifting rituals are our invitation to change gears and get off our current frequency and onto this new one. Some people adopt rituals like drinking only green tea while writing, wearing a particular hat when presenting, or doing neck rolls and yawning at the same time (this works quite well!). Find a ritual that clicks with you, and form it into a habit that you perform when shifting gears.

Rituals are established, predictable, patterned behaviors that structure us. We need structure to achieve goals because it allows for more flow.

Rituals allow us to build upon our creativity by freeing us from the perils of distractions. They act as vital partners along our journey to organize by setting our internal clocks and guiding us from one path to the other with their signals. Through them, we are able to charge our activities with renewed clarity.

Tip #5: Discover Time-Wasters

Why are we not productive? Very simple question, and often times results in an even more simple answer. We are wasting time on things that steal our energy, our motion, and our attention.

Diversion is a terrible coping mechanism. Not unlike a river, when we divert our focus to other things, we are only clearing the paths as we wait for more opportune moments to get us back to where we know we need to be. Just as a river's natural tendency is powerful, so too are we. Water needs to flow, and will seek the path of least resistance to do so. If we divert it away from its natural path, it will follow. It will rip through whatever it must to stay in motion because water must have room. The problem with diversion is that there are consequences to this action. The path left behind now has to deal with the ramifications of having no water. The plants on it may die. The wildlife that once fed off its rich eco-system may risk starvation.

The Natural Flow

When we block flow, we risk the death of possibility.

If you've got a dream and divert your attention away from that dream to deal with something outside its needs, you may be putting it in harm's way. The more you divert your attention away from your goals, the less likely you are to achieve them. You will offer life and sustenance to something outside the scope of what's important to you instead. Meanwhile, your dream shrivels up, scorched from the lack of vital attention it needs to survive.

If you're serious about getting more productive, you have to find out what diverts your attention and stop it in its tracks. You have to take stock in those things within your control to get ahead of the tidal wave that is capable of drowning out your dreams.

Wasting Time is a Habit

Habits are those things we do without having to think about them. The more you escape into them, the easier it is to say no to what's important and say yes to those escapes.

To break the habit of wasting time, you've got to be aware you are giving in to a bad habit, and then be willing to change that.

How? An effective way of overcoming a bad habit is to replace it with a good one. Think of someone who strives to overcome the bad habit of smoking. To just cut it out is very hard. If you replace the activity of smoking with a good habit, say taking a brisk walk instead of a smoke break, you are giving yourself something positive on which to focus, and your chance of success increases dramatically.

Time wasters sneak in like algae and eat up your vital resources. Learn to recognize them so they have no power.

Common Time Wasters

Interruptions

You're in the zone, typing away at a report that, if done correctly, will set you on a course to reach the next rung on the ladder of your success. You're deep in thought, typing with precise fluency, creating solutions to problems with each keystroke. Then, a knock on the door comes. A colleague sticks her head in your office. "I'm going downstairs to get some coffee. Come with me." You look up from your masterpiece and into her waiting eyes. The flow comes to a sudden halt, dying right there at your fingertips. She's just destroyed your current path and diverted it down an alternate one that will take you away from where you need to be.

Solution:

If you have an office, put a note on your door. "Do not disturb. I will be available at 10 a.m." If you are in a cubicle, block the entrance of it, and attach the same note. Also, put on a set of headphones. Also, turn off email and social media alerts.

Lured by play time

Let's face it, playing outdoes hard work in the fun department. Who wouldn't rather escape into a good book or movie, play a video game, or listen to music instead of directing the brain on an activity that requires intense focus and discipline?

We are going to have temptations pop up in our environments because we don't live on deserted islands and take naps under coconut trees. We live in a world chocked full of technology and sweet treats. So, to help protect your flow, set yourself up for success by creating a system that works to keep you on the right track.

Solution:

Set a timer and work without a break for 20-50 minute intervals. Once you've completed the time goal, set the timer again. Allow yourself to play for 10-20 minutes. Keep repeating this until you complete the task. If a timer doesn't work, set your standard by a task. Break up your work for the day into small tasks. When you complete one task, take a break for 20 minutes, then go back and do the next task.

Our brains love this kind of structure and reward system.

Email

For some reason, we feel the need to respond to people right away. If someone emails us, we're compelled to stop what we're doing and get them the answer they seek. Pride surges in us, perhaps because we've squashed a potential task item before it had the chance of landing on our plate. Or maybe we want to appear eager and available. Regardless of the reason, whenever we stop to check email, we divert our attention from the task at hand.

Solution:

Turn off email alerts. Check email on a schedule. Maybe it's once an hour, three times a day or after completing a task.

Smartphone

Unless you turn your phone off, you will be distracted by it. It will buzz. It will light up. It will do all sorts of things to take your mind off what you are trying to get accomplished. When we get alerted, we want to glance down and see what's happening. It's human nature to want to stay informed. In a report published in the Journal of Experimental Psychology: Human Perception and Performance, researchers from Florida State University found that even if you don't look at your phone when it buzzes, the sound pulls you away. (Stothart, Mitchum, & Yehnert, August 2015)

Solution:

Put your phone away when going into the zone. Simple. Check it once you're clear and out of the zone.

Social media

This creates a huge problem for many. The lure of social media drives many out of control. When I first started out as a published author, I set up my social media profiles. I was addicted to Facebook and Twitter. I checked my profiles all the time. I looked at Facebook first thing upon waking and last thing before going to sleep. I wanted to be in the know, so I stayed very close to the source at all times. Maybe the high of instant gratification compelled me to look at my profiles, whatever the reason, it cost me big time. My attention span took a nosedive, resulting in getting less done and delaying project completions.

Trying to get into a creative zone to write a novel takes HUGE effort and focus. The second I allowed myself a glance at social media, the flow stopped. It took another ten minutes to get back into the state of writing. I eventually got smart and put myself on a schedule, realizing the world would not end if I didn't see the Facebook comments on a picture of my sweet dog, Bumblebee, as soon as they were posted. Those comments are still going to be there whether I check them right away or check them on a pre-planned time table.

This need to be in constant response mode

threatens to kill dreams. We've set response expectations too high, in my opinion, and that's wasteful and costly.

Solution:

Create social media check-in schedule and stick to it.

Tip #6: Develop Self-Control

Self-control builds the foundation of focus and productivity. Mastering it is tricky because at every turn of the head, something or someone demands to take the driver's wheel and steer us away from our intended path.

We all know what happens when someone else drives, we become the passive passenger just along for the ride. We go where someone else takes us. We put them in charge of our plans, our safety, and ultimately our life when we fail to practice self-control.

Lack of Self-Control Destroys Productivity

What happens to us psychologically when we lose control? A dark and looming cloud composed of a sense of failure floats in and hangs out above our heads, reminding us we didn't succeed at keeping ourselves on track.

Talk about a derailment!

When someone's goal is to work out five times a week, and she works out Sunday, then takes off the next three days, working out on that fourth day seems pointless. She's failed herself. She asks herself, *why bother? I messed up. I didn't get in the five days. I may as well take it easy the rest of this week and start new next week.*

This woman has taken four steps back and one step forward. Not exactly a great thing when you're setting out to do something important for yourself.

So, here's the thing to remember, you are going to mess up from time to time. It's okay. Stop beating yourself up. Acknowledge the feelings, then snap out of it by changing your perspective on what you can do to correct it. Learn the lesson, forgive yourself, and move forward. That's the path to true redemption. Admit your faults, then take action to prove you are a willing player in the game to win.

Self-control is the ability to resist temptation. Let's look at some ways you can improve your ability to look away from those lures and stay focused on your plan.

Remember that self-control is a skill
This means you can learn it and refine it. As with any skill, you have to practice what you learn. It may not sit right in you at first, but with persistent effort at mastering it, it will find a groove and settle in like a comfy set of pajamas.

Visualize the desired result
Anytime we toss ourselves into a battle between wants and can't haves, acute pain can sweep in and knock us off our axis and have us pleading for mercy. It's in those times that we need to find a good enough reason that will sustain our will power. On our travels, temptations are going to run out in front of us and try to yank us away from our path to get on theirs. A person can power through this by blurring out the pain and shifting the focus to what's on the

other side of it. What are you trying to accomplish? Decide on your "why". If it's strong enough, it will keep you safe along the journey.

Be aware of your triggers

Self-awareness is the key to staying in control. Know your tendencies. What sets you off? What habits always win? Know ahead of time what derails you, and plan your reaction to those situations. With a solid plan going in, you're more apt to counter it and walk away undeterred.

Exercise your control

Exercise mindfulness through meditation. Simple deep breathing and refocusing your brain on those breaths can help you build will power and self-control, and increase your brain's ability to resist impulsive behaviors. Just a few minutes a day can make a significant difference. When you're faced with temptation, deep breathing is a fantastic way to set you back to focus. Or try blinking your eyes ten times in a row.

Get rid of the statement *I can't*

Research has shown that when we state "I can't," we are creating a dangerous feedback loop that reminds us of our inadequacies. Our brains then go on a hunt to ensure we are not wrong, which results in self-sabotage. Change your statement to something more affirmative. So, say you're trying to lose ten pounds for an upcoming wedding, and you're facing a plate of cookies. Instead of saying "I can't resist them," try saying instead, "I don't eat cookies." This affirmative statement put you in control instead. It's your choice. You are not forcing yourself to resist something, instead you are choosing to resist something.

Tip #7: Set Goals

If you're going to take a big road trip from one end of America to the other, you're likely not going to just jump in the car on a whim, accelerate down the road, and drive with blinders on towards the west without a plan, right?

You're going to plan a few things. You'll sit down and figure out what you need to bring with you to thrive on this trip. For me, that includes nuts and chocolate and, of course, a road trip wouldn't be complete without a family-sized bag of Cheetos.

You're also likely to plot out some points you want to stop at along the way. For instance, if you've always wanted to see the Empire State Building in New York City, you'll have to concede on a few things when driving to make sure perhaps you take a slight detour North, then East to get there.

Most everything in life veers far from a straight shot in any one direction. You're going to have those moments in life when you need to go up, down, or even backwards to reach a goal. The goal being in this case, a road trip that eventually leads west to where you've visualized all the places you've dreamed of visiting. To reach that dream, you need to set goals. New York City is just one goal along the journey.

A Map

If you don't know where you're going, it's going to be harder to get there. You're going to get sidetracked. You're going to risk losing sight of the big picture of what you're trying to accomplish because life is full of distraction.

There are times when losing yourself in the beauty of the open road is a wonderful and necessary thing to do. Right now though, I'm talking about your big dreams and getting there. You don't want to leave your big dreams up to luck or whim. You want to plot your points and ensure you're taking the necessary steps to get past obstacles, twists, and distractions.

When you set goals, you are in effect holding yourself accountable. You have something very specific you are aiming at, and this helps to cue you in to specific actions that need to be taken to firm up your aim.

Set Your Eyes on the Prize

Most people tend to work harder when they set their eyes on something in the distance. Take a runner in a 10K race. Those mile markers along the race trail keep her going. She sees that she's accomplished kilometer marker one, then two, then three, and so on. She can mentally check these off as accomplished, which in turn grants her empowerment and a progressive outlook. When she finally sees that beautiful finish line in front of her, with all those spectators clapping and cheering her on, something magical happens. She focuses in on that finish line and uses it as fuel to get her past the ache in her legs and the burning in her lungs, as she opens up her stride and keeps all of her efforts to the very end.

Her plotted goals (marked kilometers) kept her in check and informed. She knew exactly where she stood in the grand scheme of her dream (to cross the finish line). That know-how kept her going, kept her pushing, kept her in alignment with her plans.

With any big dream, having already plotted these points along the way keeps things focused and productive. When you know what needs to be done, your vision clears and your energy paces itself more efficiently.

If you want to see circles, stop looking for squares.

Create S.M.A.R.T. Goals

S.M.A.R.T. goals are: Specific, Measurable, Attainable, Realistic and Time-Based.

S – Specific. Ask yourself *who, what, when, where and why*.

M – Measurable. You want to be able to measure your achievements. Often times, people create vague goals like *I want to increase my cash flow.* How will you know when your cash flow has been adequately increased? Instead rewrite this goal to be *I want to increase my cash flow by 5% by the end of this fiscal year.* Now, you can measure the results with precision.

A – Attainable. Be sure the goals you set are something you can achieve without killing yourself. Remember you want to set yourself up for success with them. You must be able to control the outcome of the goal on your own, too. If you rely on certain conditions in the market to achieve your goal, you're just partaking in wishful thinking.

R – Realistic. Be sure to set goals that are achievable. If you want to become a doctor in under a year, you're going to fail. If you want to become the next big icon in the music industry in a year, you might be stretching it, or not. Stretch yourself, but in a realistic sense. All things take time.

T – Time-based. Set a deadline to keep that engine firing. When you know you have a certain amount of time to get it done, you're going to do everything you can to safeguard that you take that time and use it wisely. Is someone depending on you to complete a goal? Is there an event that is going to take place, and you need to complete your goal by then? Excuses have no place when you've set up a deadline for yourself or have committed to one set by others.

Example of a S.M.A.R.T. and Not-So-Smart Goal

Not so smart: – "I will exercise more."
S.M.A.R.T. – "This month, I will take a brisk walk five times a day for thirty minutes at a time."

This is very specific, measurable, attainable,

realistic, and time-based.

Is Your Goal Important Enough?

Again, this goes back to knowing your priorities, and knowing how those priorities fit into your big dream. When you can say that a goal is necessary to the overall success of fitting into your priorities and thus big dream, then you've got a great goal.

Too often people set goals that have nothing to do with the big picture of their life. You should want to achieve it. That desire is your motivation. If you just think you should achieve it because you know it's what's expected of you, the drive will dissipate and sputter out over time. Know your priorities, and guarantee you have a strong emotional tie to them.

How Can You Achieve Your Goals?

Write them down
You want to see them. You want to review them daily. I hung a white board in my office and wrote them down on it. I review this whiteboard every day.

I know exactly what I need to accomplish, and a constant reminder of why. I love checking off a goal once it's been achieved.

Share your goals

You will place yourself in the prime position of being accountable. When you know your actions are going to be checked, you're going to push out that extra effort to be able to say at the end of the day, "Yup, I did it!"

Plot winning points

Create those kilometer markers, if you will. Decide at what point an action deserves a celebration. If a goal extends over a year period, create monthly win points along the way so empowerment can rush in and sweep you up into its arms, letting you know that you are on the right track. Visualize a long trail with rest stops. Each rest stop offers a treat.

When I was a child, my parents used to take our family on long hikes through a favorite wooded park. The hikes would sometimes extend two to three hours, climbing over tree limbs, crossing muddy trenches, and running into the occasional snake or critter. As a child with legs not quite as strong or long as my parents, these hikes would take a toll.

My parents were smart. They set up a reward system, one that always got me excited about these afternoon treks through the trees and tangled underbrush. They'd set up treat spots along the way, and once we reached them they'd dig out of their backpacks a Snickers bar for each of us. We'd sit on boulders and sink our teeth into the gooey, rich, nutty piece of heaven and savor the moment. That chocolate bar made the trek worth it. It gave me that extra push when I wanted to break out into a whine. It motivated me and made me hungry to achieve those digestible steps along the way to our goal.

Take the first step

If you are having a difficult time getting started on a goal, just take the first step. One little step can mean the difference between achieving it or not. It all starts with a step. What first step do you need to take to get started? Figure it out by listing potential tasks to achieve the goal, then start there!

To make it from point A to point B you must be willing to take a step.

Tip #8: Key in on Your Highest Value Activities

When we talk about high value activities (HVA), I'm talking about those activities that yield the highest return. These are the action items on your to-do list that will set you apart, get you to the next level, and move you closer to your end goal.

Focusing too intently on activities that aren't related to your top goal will only cause you to move further away from it. We see this all the time with people who want to be active, yet they dedicate themselves to clearing out their DVD recordings by watching marathon episodes the whole day.

I've been there. I've opted to watch hours upon hours of recordings of *American Idol* year after year while I had big projects waiting on me to get started. Watching a star be born on American television will not help me generate revenue and put food on my table. My word count for the day will not build itself. I am not going to meet new readers or score interview opportunities if I'm parked passively in front of the television watching someone else give birth to her dream.

Determine Your HVAs

If you want to get ahead and stay productive, you must determine those activities that will help move you forward. Then, you must prioritize those activities and attend to them the most.

If you're a web designer with dreams to open your own design studio, then your highest value activities should remain focused around activities that bring you increase in your knowledge, client base, and bottom line. Those activities should get precedent over anything else on your daily list. You want to focus on improving your skills in this area, always searching for new opportunities as you prepare by doing the work that will generate the level of awareness you need to succeed.

You have to figure out what activities will help you move closer and which ones are just sucking the life out of your dreams. If you want to write novels, then writing a novel should be on the top of your activities list. Too often people avoid the very thing they should be doing by adding extraneous things onto their plate, like hobbies. Hobbies should never have front row seat to your HVAs. If you enjoy playing guitar, that's great. Though, unless you dream of becoming a guitarist, put the guitar down and get started on your HVA first. The guitar riffs are a treat for after you've completed your HVAs for the day.

Blocks to HVAs

Social media poses the biggest offense to HVAs. The hours that get wasted daily on social media is absurd. As an entrepreneur it's easy to get sucked into the vortex of Facebook or Twitter. We're programmed to believe we need to be online to be noticed. We must show up and post interesting content, and offer equal attention to commenting and liking other people's posts.

When I first started publishing my books, I set up social media profiles and focused on growing them. I needed readers, so I would spend hours interacting with people from all over the world. The distraction of it derailed my efforts to get my word count goals in. I'd start writing a scene and *BAM!* a Facebook notification would pop onto my smartphone screen.

Don't get me wrong, social media is necessary in marketing as an Indie writer. But, if writing is my goal, then social media marketing must take a secondary seat to that. My HVA is writing. That needs to have its own limelight. Anything short of that is counterproductive.

It's imperative to look at your activities and determine which ones are highest value and which ones are low-yield. If it helps, think of your activities as investment vehicles. The investment is your time, energy and attention. The yield is the outcome of this investment. Be sure you are spending your time wisely on those activities that will generate the tools, knowledge, and revenue you need to sustain and increase momentum towards your dream.

By determining your HVAs, you're also defining what you should and shouldn't say no to. In a previous section we discussed the importance of being able to say no to things that take you away from your desires. When we say yes to things that are not HVAs, we are undermining our efforts and their results will not be to our advantage.

Action Steps to Help Focus on Your HVAs

Audit your to-do list
Scan your list and determine which activities are most important to your goals. Ask yourself, how will this help improve my success at achieving XYZ? Those answers should help you determine which gets moved to the top and to the bottom of your list.

Select one HVA
In your daily routine, you will have many items that aren't HVAs, but are nonetheless important and necessary to get done. Things like cleaning the

bathroom, sending your mom a quick email to let her know you love her, walking your dog, etc. Although these items aren't adding revenue to your bottom line, they are still vital to your life. That being said, when analyzing your list for HVAs, select one that you will do for each day. Don't go a day without doing at least one HVA. You may not get to all of them, but you can at least do one.

Delegate

You may find that you are bogged down with tasks that have to be done, but don't add any value to your ventures. Are there things you can delegate on your list to clear up space for your HVAs? When you clear your schedule, you open yourself up to clarity and the freedom to discover more value in your daily actions.

Tip #9: Focus on the Task at Hand

I've tried multitasking way too many times. I fail each time. You know why? Multitasking doesn't work! That's right. We are not hardwired to perform multiple tasks at the same time, contrary to popular opinion.

Multitasking decreases productivity and, take it from one who knows, it'll burn you out faster than you can count to ten at blazing speed. Not only will you burn out, but you'll likely do so without having that end result you desired in the first place.

Think about it, if you're not fully engaged in an activity, you're going to miss out on parts of it. It's a scientific fact. According to Dr. Earl Miller, Professor of Neuroscience at MIT, the brain can't process two streams of income at the same time.

(Levitin, 2015)

Multitasking Doesn't Work

Let's turn to an example to illustrate. Say you're inclined to listen to an online lecture while balancing your checkbook. Will you absorb all the critical parts of that lecture and get all the numbers crunched and balanced in one sitting? Likely, you'll find yourself frustrated to discover that you'll have to redo parts of both, creating even more of a productivity issue.

You see, your brain will only pick up one element at a time. You're just wreaking havoc on your ability to get both tasks done effectively.

When you single task, you consciously commit to giving your full attention to a given task. Do this and you're more likely to process and apply information quicker and with greater execution. By ignoring other demands, you tune in with sharper focus, enabling the opportunity to complete a task and open yourself up to new ones more efficiently.

Benefits of Single Tasking

Single tasking allows you to train your brain to focus more intently. Have you ever found yourself grappling to remember an important fact, birthday, or even someone's name? This happens when we fail to cement it to memory, and it's often due to distraction.

Single tasking is easier said than done. I get it. I often find that random important thoughts creep into my mind when I'm trying to focus. This annoys me! I'm trying to focus, yet here comes this wandering thought, barging its way in without any consideration for my efforts to stay in complete control over the task at hand!

When I'm single tasking, this is inevitable. The solution isn't to focus on abolishing the intruding thoughts (heck some of my most brilliant ideas have come in as intruders!). All that abolishing them will do is create more of a pull on your mind. Instead, try jotting those ideas down on paper and dealing with them later.

A curious thing happens when we commit our

thoughts to paper. We are able to cut the tie with them because we are smart enough to know that we have parked them for later. The fear of loss sheds and a welcoming respite from trying to save the thought replaces it.

Zap Distractions

Okay, so say you're willing to try this single tasking, but distractions still tap on your proverbial door. Well, admittedly, there will be times when we can't focus fully on a task without taking a break and dealing with a new demand. Anyone who has children or a spirited pet might understand this!

Let's just say that whenever possible, set ground rules to avoid the pitfalls of external disruptions. Place a sign on your office door. Turn off your cellphone. Close email applications. Set yourself up for success wherever and whenever possible.

That long, laundry list of must do to-do items can overwhelm, as well. And, we've all got them. Group similar tasks into a certain timeframe within the day to stay focused. For instance, if your list consists of online items, set aside ten to fifteen minutes to log in and check your social media accounts, email, text messages, etc. Grouping similar items helps you stay in a necessary task zone, and can help keep your brain on the wavelength needed to perform the tasks effectively and efficiently.

Recognize when you're multi-tasking and nip it in that moment. The sooner you build your focus, the sooner your productivity will soar and you will win on achieving your short and long term goals.

Tip #10: Think Small, Digestible Steps

Nothing screams overwhelming like a gigantic, looming task with no end in sight. When overwhelmed, you will never produce your best work. The natural response when facing an insurmountable mountain like this is to run the other way and hope for something easier. As much as you might want to toss the monster idea aside and tackle something less intimidating and immediate, the fighter in you will need a better plan.

Immediate – there's a leveraging word.

If a dream is too big to grasp, it's hard to view it in any immediate terms. So, here is where you can play a productive card in your hand and turn that enormous, scary mountain into something more digestible.

One Bite at a Time

Imagine you're staring at a plate of macaroni. If you attempted to clear your plate in one move, you'd choke. So, instead, you'd dig your fork into it and conquer one bite at a time, allowing yourself the time, space, and ability to accomplish the task at hand. Before you know it, you will start to see the plate's surface. One by one, that pile of macaroni disappears and digests, offering you more productive fuel to power your journey to the ultimate goal.

View your dreams like that macaroni. Break the enormous dream (clearing your plate) into tasks (one bite at a time), and devour them until you've succeeded.

As you start to work on your tasks, one digestible step at a time, celebrate your successes. Treat yourself when you complete a portion.

Don't Fear a Step Backwards

Don't be afraid to take a few steps backwards if you run into obstacles. Many believe that productivity means pushing forward no matter what.

That can sometimes be counterproductive if you're facing a brick wall. Often times, these brick walls offer opportunity to step back and take a look at your path to make sure it's still right for you.

If a brick wall stands in your way, instead of limiting yourself to the planned route, allow for flexibility. In fact, plan on it. You need to be flexible. Being flexible sometimes takes us off the structured path, and that's good. We often find solutions on that ground that has never seen a footprint.

To get to where you're going, you may have to take several steps backwards, giving yourself time to consider things with more creativity. Being productive has nothing to do with speed or time, but progress. Progress sometimes requires stepping back, taking in a wider view, and then getting back to the task at hand with a clearer plan of action.

Leave a Task Incomplete

If you're stuck on a task, in addition to taking in a wider view, you can also take another approach. Select the biggest tasks to complete your ultimate goal. These will become your anchors.

Here's how. Leave these incomplete, on purpose.

Say what?

Yes. When you leave tasks incomplete, your mind won't forget them. You create a cliffhanger that begs for you to go back and settle the intrigue. Not only will the cliffhanger beg for your continued attention, but it'll do something very productive. It will create opportunity for freshness to flow in because you will be figuring out how to tackle the cliffhanger in a new setting, which will allow for new perspectives.

Most of my creative ideas flow to me when I'm not in front of my computer. I love leaving a cliffhanger sentence at the end of a writing session because I contemplate how I will resolve or build upon it while I'm not in front of a blank computer screen.

Tip #11: Create a Deadline

A deadline creates a state of urgency. When we layer a project in urgency, our push to complete it strengthens.

When we know we have a surplus of time on our hands, we tend to take it for granted. Think of a lazy day when hours upon hours stretch before you with not an iota of plans squeezed into them. Most of us, if answering honestly, would admit that we take our sweet time getting anything done. We may delay getting out of bed, enjoying the soft plush of comfort enveloping us in those early morning hours when we'd typically jump out of bed and get to work.

We may lounge over a second or third cup of coffee instead of showering after breakfast. We may decide that the movie playing on our television is much more interesting to commit to than the toilet and sink we had planned to clean. By mid-afternoon, we'd likely find ourselves ditching the grocery shopping and just ordering in a pizza, covering up under a warm blanket, and watching marathon shows of our favorite sitcom until the sun goes down.

Who can blame a person for such indulgence?

We do need some flexibility and downtime. These are those hours in the day that are sacred and allow for breathing room. They must be kept separate. When it's time to relax – relax. When it's time to produce – produce.

A State of Urgency

A state of urgency will get you through those moments when you are challenged, overwhelmed, or under a cloud of banal nothingness. We all have those moments when we want to toss a project out the window and bury our heads in a pillow.

There are times in life when we need to get our butts in gear and get to work. If we quit every time the going got tough, we'd end up on a dead-end street frustrated that we can't move forward.

Sometimes this state of urgency will come in the form of self-imposed deadlines or external ones. No matter their form, the need for immediate action is powerful in creating the kind of momentum that can move mountains.

Create Markers

I remember a while back taking a fitness class, and the instructor charged us with remaining in a plank position for a full minute. Most of us groaned and wanted to fall on our bellies after twenty seconds, until she yelled out "You can do anything for 60 seconds. It's just 60 short seconds. Now get there."

Her words dove deep. She not only got me to that sixty second mark that day, but she also, without her knowledge, continues to get me through moments in life when it would be much easier to just fall on my belly and give up. I hear her voice when I am stuck in the middle of writing a novel with no solid direction, when I am a mile into a long-distance run and want to take a walk break, and when I'd rather spend my day lounging instead of tackling a task towards my goal.

She introduced me to the tool of markers.

You see, when you break time down into increments that are realistic and measurable, you create a marker in your brain that gets you over those annoying humps. Those markers, those deadlines, help generate the extra push we need to stay the course and put in that extra hour or two. When something is important to you, laziness has no place. You do what you have to do to get it done.

When you know something has to get done at a certain time, you are more apt to produce more in less time, and end on a quality note. This is because you force your brain into focus, and whenever in focus, you're going to get the answers you seek, solve the problems that arise, and get more creative. If you focus for two days to find a solution to a complex problem, you're not going to slack and wreak havoc on yourself. No, you're going to put your mind to the test and force it to shut down unnecessary functions so you can save all the energy for the task at hand. You're going to say no to that happy hour. You're not going to sit down on the couch and veg out to reruns of *Friends* or *The Big Bang Theory*. You're going to get the work done.

Another thing happens when we have too much time. We tend to over-analyze our actions. This can derail us and stop momentum. With too much time to think of every possible angle, we're not likely to exert influential strides and present our final project with the confidence we would've, had we trusted our instincts and training. Instead of allowing stress to highlight the results, allow it to highlight the deadline. A little anxiety can be a good catalyst to progress.

Tip #12: Nurture Your Health

One of my top priorities in life is to guard my health. Without it, I'm going to have a very hard time getting anything done.

We can control taking care of ourselves. We can choose wisely.

It goes without saying that eating healthy and getting adequate exercise is the key to maintaining a healthy lifestyle. When we feed our bodies the proper nutrients and work it out the way it needs, it operates at its greatest potential.

If we put bad fuel into our car gas tank, our car will sputter and the engine will eventually lose its power and ability to keep us moving. The same is true of our body. If we fill it with garbage, it's going to flake out on us over time. We're not going to be as vibrant as we can be to do great work.

If we fail to water a plant, it will die. Its leaves will shrivel up, turn brown, and fall off. It needs nurturing. It needs care. It needs the proper nutrients to keep its leaves green.

Health is Required to Stay at Peak

Many people argue that it's impossible to fit health into their schedule. They've got too many demands pulling at them to take an hour each day to prepare healthy meals and get in a workout.

Though true, many of us are overworked and overscheduled, that is our choice. We can choose to reevaluate our commitments. We can choose to put our health in the list of our top priorities, and in so doing, we will have to shed other things. If you analyze the other things taking up time, you may find that they are time wasters. An hour of television here and there appears innocent enough. Add those up at the end of a week and see how much time you have collected.

Living a healthy lifestyle is a matter of choice.

You have to decide that it's important enough to you and your family, and then find ways to guarantee success.

The choice should be easy if you look at the benefits of a healthy lifestyle.

Exercise helps your brain grow

Your brain is a muscle. The more you work it out, the stronger it becomes. The more you use it, the more it grows. When we exercise, we affect our brain. It lights up areas that do important work. Exercise stimulates, which means it helps keep your brain in constant growth mode.

Health offers clarity

The cleaner your fuel, the cleaner your system. When your blood vessels are in a prime state, the flow is strong. Your body gets the fuel it needs to function at its highest level. Your brain gets the nutrients it needs to perform and feed your organs the vital energy they need to run properly. When your brain gets what it needs, it will stay clear and focused, allowing you to get things done efficiently and effectively.

A positive outlook

When you exercise, your brain releases feel-good chemicals, resulting in a positive outlook on the various aspects of your life. When you're happy, productivity rises because you are not bogged down with stress, aggression, frustration, or any other negative vibe.

Energy surge

Exercise and good nutrition boosts your energy level, increasing your alertness and decision-making abilities. You are able to adapt to changing or stressful situations.

Bottom line, when you feel your best, things just flow better. You can focus more sharply. Your energy increases. You're happier. You're free!

Feeling your best doesn't require schemes and crazy concoctions. You won't have to exercise two hours every day, eat flavorless food, and forgo all fun in pursuit of it. Just a few simple tweaks and additions can get you feeling fantastic.

I've experimented with many steps to improve my health.

My Top 9 Favorite Health Tips

Get in Extra Steps
If you work in an office building, take the steps instead of the elevator. If you drive into work, park your car at the far end of the parking lot. Every step counts!

Drink lemon water
Lemon water flushes out toxins and is beneficial for the body. It tastes delicious nice and warm first thing in the morning. It cleanses and hydrates.

Alkalize
Too much acid can wreak havoc on the immune system, creating an imbalance. Eat foods high in alkaline to counter this. Foods I enjoy in this group

are lemons, watermelon, pineapple, apple cider vinegar, seaweed, raisins, and kale... to name a few.

Take a probiotic

Probiotics can improve intestinal function and maintain the integrity of the lining of the gut. There's also lots of evidence that probiotics help maintain a strong immune system. A lot of health issues start in the gut; a probiotic can be helpful in improving digestive health. (Always consult a medical expert if you are unsure if a supplement is right for you.)

Forgive

Letting go of bitterness can restore peace and balance. I'm guilty of holding onto anger and frustration over the actions of others. You'll never hear me tell you that any such grudge has ever served me in a positive way. The moment we forgive, we free ourselves. Oftentimes, we save ourselves more than the person we are forgiving.

Admit when you're wrong

When pride stands in the way, relationships can suffer. Letting go of it can free us to enjoy those we love. Admitting I'm wrong has never come easy for me, especially if the other person is just as wrong. I can be stubborn! I find it amazing though, each and every time I apologize first, the air becomes lighter, the weight drops from my shoulders, and I can draw a deep, soulful breath. I love when the apology is offered, and the other person opens up and shares an equally heartfelt one too. Of course, a reciprocated apology doesn't always happen. When it doesn't I know deep down that I still need to be okay with admitting I was wrong. Admittedly, when I know the other party is just as wrong, this can be difficult to do. But, I also know that by opening up the lines of communication, growth has a chance of happening.

Stretch

Stretching has many benefits. Some include: relief from pain, improved posture, and greater sense of well-being. Even five minutes a day can heighten your joy. Can't find five extra minutes? Stretch in between work tasks, or while performing routine tasks like cooking dinner brushing your teeth.

Share a smile

Smiling releases endorphins, the same feel good chemicals that are released when you exercise. I love seeing the surprise on people's faces when I break out into a smile as I walk past. A lot of times, they look at me like I just landed from another planet. Most of the time, though, they reciprocate.

Compliment someone

If you like someone's shirt, let her know. If someone is smiling, thank her for spreading it to you. Small, little compliments turn into huge spirit boosts for both you and the person receiving. You increase positivity, open yourself up to receive happiness, and it's FUN!

Allow for the rest in between hard work. Recharging is necessary and should never be viewed as a waste of time in the pursuit of progress.

Tip #13: Take a Nap

This might sound like a counterintuitive idea, but much research points to the validity of taking naps to help us become more productive and alert.

Right as I sat down to write this portion of the book, my energy flaked out. The coffee from the morning had long left my system, and I had just finished eating rice and chicken for lunch. I set a timer for ten minutes (a ritual I do to fill a blank screen with something, anything to get me in flow), and wouldn't you know, my eyes began to lower and my brain whispered, *absolutely, no way are we doing this right now.* So, I did what I am suggesting to anyone who experiences similar lag, I took a quick nap.

Now, I am wide awake and the creativity is

flowing.

I know taking a nap is not always, if ever, a convenient thing. Many people don't have a quiet, private place to seal off from the world for ten to fifteen minutes. If you do have privacy, buy a yoga mat and have it handy. If you work in a busy environment without four walls and a locked door, then get creative. If you drive into work, perhaps take your lunch break in your car. If that's not an option, find a quiet spot in a break room and lay your head on the table. Think safety first, of course. Know your surroundings, and only nap where you can safely close your eyes and not have to be on alert.

Why Nap?

Researchers have conducted many experiments that have revealed sleep improves learning, memory, alertness, and creative thinking.

Additionally, according to Harvard sleep researcher, Robert Stickgold, napping enhances problem-solving skills, even helping people to separate important information from extraneous details. (Harvard, 2009)

Even the National Sleep Foundation recommends napping twenty to thirty minutes to improve alertness and performance. They also say that these short naps will not leave you groggy or interfere with your nighttime sleep. (NSF, 2016)

Another great benefit of napping is that it can help prevent burnout. We live in a time when we are urged to always push the go button. This can have dangerous consequences on our health and safety. We are not programmed to go without rests. If we do, we end up being cranky, restless, frustrated fools running around in circles and going nowhere fast.

Our Brains Need Time to Recharge

Our bodies need time to settle down. Our hearts need time to slow down. The action of napping can help us achieve these vital needs.

Napping is like a computer reboot. You know how your computer gets bogged down with processes over time, and by shutting it down, you give it a chance to recalibrate itself and align all the functions in their proper order? Napping is our body's way of rebooting itself, recalibrating, and getting realigned.

I have this strong visual of myself without regular naps that scares the crapola out of me. I imagine my brain short-circuiting and leaking toxic waste from the misfires into my bloodstream where it then begins to erode my veins and disintegrate my bones like battery acid would. I then, picture smoke billowing out of my ears, eyes, and mouth, like I'm on fire and ready to explode.

Maybe it's my massive fear of burning in a fire that creates this terrible visual. Whatever the cause, it works for me. I do not want to short circuit my brain. I love my brain and want to take very good care of it. It's the only one I'm going to get, and so I nurture it as I would a newborn baby. I rest it when it needs rest, and I work it when I know it needs to work. I feed it the foods that increase its happy vibe, pretty much anything alive that grows from Mother Earth. I exercise it frequently to reward it with the edge it craves.

Our brains are sharp, and if we treat them with the love they deserve, they'll thrive. Napping is one of the greatest gifts you can offer your brain. That midday boost will help it to focus and take you places only a healthy, vibrant brain can.

Tip #14: Find the Key Ingredient

To be productive, you've got to be in a great state of mind. You cannot circle around this and expect a different fact. You can't be running a million miles an hour and expect to notice the important details along the roadside. You're going to miss them when going at that blazing speed. The same concept maintains itself when your mind is a million miles away from where you're present. You're going to miss those small innuendos that are there to guide and inspire.

If you're planning dinner while you're sipping on your morning smoothie, you're going to miss the freshness of the healthy greens and sweetness of the frozen fruit as it dances on your tongue and slips away past your taste buds. If you're mulling over how you will tackle the laundry and get the kids off to soccer on time while you're sitting in a work meeting, you're going to miss out on information that may make or break a project.

Be in the Moment

When you're elsewhere, you're not being productive and moving towards your dreams. You're falling down the long, dark abyss of missed opportunities.

An important element of success is lost when you're not focused on the present. Experiencing joy in your projects is what breathes life into your dreams and helps you to stay present. Without joy, little will get you through those moments when challenges set in and doom corners you at every turn. It's the joy of the journey that fires up your passion and keeps you putting one foot in front of the other, at times trudging, and other times leaping to get to the next bend in the road.

Where skills and abilities fail, joy and passion kick in. They can be the catalyst to great advance and the secret to your ultimate success. When you're in a state of joy, you don't want to escape the moment. Rather, you clasp onto that prize, not wavering from its poignant and rich presence. You want to keep it sacred, protecting it with your nurturing love to ensure its survival.

Joy Makes Everything Work Better

Deals come through. People act more amenable. Obstacles roll off to the side. If a mountain appears before you, you view it not as a blockage, but as a wonderful chance to climb to its summit and view the world like you've never viewed it before.

The greatest thing you can do on pursuit to your dreams is search for that joy like you're on the hunt for survival. It is the key to staying in the game and winning.

Stress can't exist on the same field as joy. Worry and anxiety will not be able to dig their claws into your journey because joy will snuff them out. You will not worry about the past or future because you're living in the moment. That moment is where great strides take place. Every beat of the heart creates more joy, which fuels every step forward, every breath you draw. In those movements, momentum builds, and this momentum will take you places stress and dissatisfaction never can.

Joy Nurtures Focus

When you're staring at a beautiful sunset, you are in tune with its energy. Nothing else matters. Because you are so immersed in the beauty that graces your view, you couldn't care less about anything outside of that experience.

This is the zone you want to be in when you're working on your dreams. You want to be sitting before that sunset in awe, taking in nothing else but the dazzling insights, lessons, and growth it offers your soul.

When in the zone, your desires, skills, and magnificent brain bond and conspire to push you forward and create great things. You're in flow. You lose yourself in the work. Time doesn't matter in this magical flow.

When you're this happy, you won't want to leave. That is the secret to productivity, find the key and gain access to the flow. You can't get there or stay there if you keep switching your mind to the past or the future, worrying about what already happened and what will be. The only way to stay in flow is to zero in on what gets your heart smiling, then do it.

The Challenge of Getting into Flow

Getting into this state of flow can be challenging at first. Your mind wants to wander. It wants to stick to its habits, which in most cases has a firm grip on multitasking, overanalyzing the past and overthinking the future. Be patient with yourself as you're learning to get in flow. Experiment to find what turns on your happy vibe. Most of us are so busy trying to catch up or get ahead that we don't take the time to figure out the source of our joy. We settle on jobs and social situations that are comfortable and safe, never exploring life outside the boundaries we've imposed on ourselves.

I had no idea how joyful oil painting could be

until I experimented with taking a class delivered through our local county parks and recreation department. I saw the course listed, and thought, *that looks like fun.* So, I signed up. My instructor assigned me the task of painting a replica of an oil painting that I found in a book or on a website. So, I choose a William Michael Harnett painting of a violin. Guided by a very patient teacher, I let go of fears of embarrassment and failure and just slipped into a creative space where time had no factor.

Absorbed in the moment, my focus zoomed in on that canvas and I got lost in a wondrous zone where I wanted to snuggle up and stay for as long as possible. Being in the zone parallels to what a first deep breath would be to someone close to drowning. The freedom and gratitude superseded any stress, worry or further desire to escape that distinct moment of realizing I was truly alive.

If you don't know what this feeling is, take the time to discover it for yourself. With it, you will have access to all the focus you need to push those dreams forward.

When I am stumbling over words in a chapter I am writing, I turn to my brushes, paint and canvas and lose myself. That state of relaxation allows my brain to reset and recharge, and by the time I'm back to writing, I'm clear-headed and creative again, focused on the magic of writing and not the stress of dealing with writer's block.

There is an activity out there to tickle everyone's heart. You just have to be willing to dig around and uncover yours.

When you are in the zone, you are present. When you're present, you're aligned to focus.

Tips to Staying Present:

Do one thing at a time
If you're ironing clothes, just iron clothes. If you're driving a car, just drive the car. If you're eating a salad, just eat the salad.

Get your senses involved
Experience the full range of sensory details around

you. How does that iron feel in your hands? What does the steam smell like? Watch the wrinkles smooth out over your fabric. While driving, enjoy the rough texture of the steering wheel as it presses against the palms of your hand. Listen to the engine hum. When eating that salad, enjoy the crunch of the lettuce and cucumbers and the sweet taste they create when they blend together into a delightful nutritious cocktail that brings you vitality.

The more you practice focusing, the better you will be at it.

Be aware

You will have moments when your mind wanders. Recognize what is happening. Being aware is crucial. You will have times when you need to go over past events to learn lessons and you will have to think future potentials through to make informed decisions. Just recognize when these thoughts are interfering with your focus and productivity. Set time aside to contemplate about them later, after you've completed the task at hand.

Go into Zen mode

Sometimes just sitting still and breathing is the simplest approach to being present. In this world of high-capacity work overload, we rarely take time to just be. Guilt shreds us if we're not running around accomplishing something concrete, forgetting that oftentimes, it's in the recharge where we gain the energy to stay most productive.

Get the heart pumping

Nothing breaks through the stress monster's resilience like good old-fashioned exercise. Everyone has moments when thoughts circle our brain like they are trying to create a whirlpool and drown us in their current. When this happens, it's often necessary to take out the big guns to defend against the storm surges of stress. Jumping jacks, running up and down a few flights of stairs, or taking a brisk walk can help cut the power on that whirlpool and bring things back to a nice calm level.

Tip #15: Know Your "Why"

To stay in the game, you should know why you're in it in the first place.

Do you know your "why"? One of the greatest things you can do for yourself is to take the time to figure out why you want to do the things you want to do. In those moments of weakness that will undoubtedly creep into your life at the most inopportune moments, knowing your "why" can be the difference between giving up and pushing forward.

Ask Thought-Provoking Questions

I want to share a personal experience that propelled me to take a good, hard look at why I write. I asked myself:

- What if no one reads this?
- Is all of this hard work and sacrifice worth it?
- Should I be spending my time doing something that will offer me a more secure flow of income?
- Am I being selfish by taking time away from my loved ones to hibernate for hours on end, typing a story that may never spread across the pages of a book?

Most every person has a similar set of questions she asks herself when faced with obstacles along the path of her dreams.

I certainly did. In fact, I almost quit writing altogether because I didn't know how to answer these questions.

Several years back, after writing my third novel, *Tangerine Twist*, and after having it and my other two novels, *The Fiche Room* and *Two Feet off the Ground*, rejected by countless publishers, I sat with two of my friends and announced I would quit writing.

I was done.

I worked for almost five years writing those three books, sacrificing time, money, and emotions for what?

Under a blanket of stars, I sat on their patio and told them about the rejection letter I had received that afternoon for *Tangerine Twist*. The publisher told me it didn't fit their needs – the impersonal sentence every writer dreads.

I sulked like someone just cut off my legs and told me I'd have to crawl around for the rest of my life.

My emotions flooded my brain that night. I couldn't see past the riptide pulling me under, or ignore the pounding of rocks against my naked soul.

I sat before my friends, half a glass of wine in hand, as a washed-up writer. And, darn it, I hadn't even taken my first baby step into the land of rejection!

The life of pursuing a dream can be brutal. It can wreak havoc on our emotions, causing us to sit like dried-up rotted logs on the side of a churning oceanfront if we let it.

If we let it. That's key.

In my case, I needed to get a grip, and fast.

Thankfully, I had a set of loyal friends who talked some sense into me. They stared at me with frank eyes and asked me:

- Do you write because you enjoy it?
- Do you feel excited when you write?
- Even if you inspired one person by your words, wouldn't that be enough of a reason to continue?

Find the Answers

These questions got me searching for answers.

My answer to all of those questions was yes. YES. I have stories to tell. So many I wish I had fifty hours a day to write them.

Just because a bunch of publishers rejected my books didn't mean my life as a would-be writer should die. Who were they to have such power over my future?

I had dug out a grave and tossed myself into it before I even weighed my options.

What happened in the moments following this new energy surge changed the course of my life. I'm going to quote one of my all-time favorite motivational speakers, Les Brown, to explain the prominent thought lifting me to my feet that night on my friends' patio and raising up my half glass of wine. "It's not over until I say it's over."

Later that night, I went home and formed a mission statement, or in other words, my "why". I've tweaked it over the years because I've changed and grown from that person. Back then it looked something like this: As long as I encourage, inspire and enrich at least one individual with each story I write, then I will stay committed to this unique and exciting path I'm fortunate enough to be on.

My revised one is much shorter and on point with my path today: **Learn it. Share it.**

Knowing my "why", which for me draws upon my love of learning and sharing, puts to rest any question of my purpose or reason for investing my time and energy in writing.

Remember this: If your mission is personal and rooted in something greater than money, success will have a great chance of finding you.

Find the true meaning behind what you're doing and all will align properly and shine light on your actions.

Conclusion

Congrats on taking this important step in learning how to stay focused, productive, and get things done! If you've got a compelling dream that you want to see come to fruition, you owe it to yourself to do what it takes to create opportunity.

Remember that you were put here to thrive, not just survive. You are meant for greatness.

Never stop looking for opportunities to get out of your comfort zone and stretch beyond your current circumstances. Be willing to change and tweak, and look for ways to refine your process as you learn better ways of doing things.

If you can figure out how to tap into your potential, you will experience that magical vibe of being in alignment with your life purpose.

Now you're armed with information. It's time to

buckle down, roll up your sleeves, and get it done.

I wish you an enjoyable journey as you discover many gems along the way to your dreams. And if you get stuck along the way, I welcome you to discuss your ideas with me. Come join me on Twitter or Facebook.

To learn more in-depth tips on other areas of motivation, come join me on my personal development blog, curveswelcome.com, where I post new ideas weekly. In this blog, I explore many topics around life's curves.

Thank you for your time. It's been a true pleasure.

NOTE FROM SUZIE CARR

As with all of my books, I enjoy giving a portion of proceeds back to the community by donating to the NOH8 Campaign www.noh8campaign.com and Hearts United for Animals www.hua.org. Thank you for being a part of this special contribution.

A SPECIAL REQUEST

If you enjoyed this book, I'd be so grateful for your honest review of it. Just a sentence or two will help others discover it and help me to serve you better with future books!
(www.amazon.com/author/suziecarr)

Works Cited

Harvard. (2009, November). *Napping may not be such a no-no*. Retrieved from Harvard Health Letter: http://www.health.harvard.edu/newsletter_article/napping-may-not-be-such-a-no-no

Levitin, D. J. (2015, January 18). *The Guardian*. Retrieved from The Guardian: https://www.theguardian.com/science/2015/jan/18/modern-world-bad-for-brain-daniel-j-levitin-organized-mind-information-overload

NSF. (2016). *National Sleep Foundation*. Retrieved from Napping: https://sleepfoundation.org/sleep-topics/napping

Stothart, C., Mitchum, A., & Yehnert, C. (August 2015). The attentional cost of receiving a cell phone notification. . *Journal of Experimental Psychology: Human Perception and Performance*.

Index

Action steps, 69
Boundaries, 18-19
Clarity, 89-90
Clutter, 7-12
Deadlines, 82
Delegate, 70
Distractions, 74-75
Diversion, 37
Email, 42
Frugal, 12
Get uncomfortable, 25
Goal setting, 56-63
Guilt, 20-21
Habit, 39
Health, 87-94
HVAs, 65-70
In the moment, 104
Incomplete task, 79-80
Interruptions, 40
Luck, 1
Markers, 85

Multi-tasking, 72-73
Napping, 97-101
Perfection, 29-30
Positive outlook, 90
Recharging, 99-101
Recycle, 10
Rituals, 31-34
Rules, 21
Saying yes, 15-16
Self-control, 47-50
Selfish, 17-18
Single-tasking, 73-74
Small steps, 77-78
Smartphones, 43
Social media, 43-45
Step backwards, 78-79
Task shifting, 34-35
Triggers, 50
Urgency, 82-83
Visualize, 49
Wasting time, 39-40

www.ingramcontent.com/pod-product-compliance
Lightning Source LLC
Chambersburg PA
CBHW031400040426
42444CB00005B/368